The Low Light Fight – Shooting, Tactics, Combatives

Michael R. Seeklander

Shooting-Performance

Owasso, Oklahoma

Michael R. Seeklander
P.O. Box 2016
Owasso, Ok 74055
www.shooting-performance.com

Book Layout ©2013 BookDesignTemplates.com
The Low Light Fight-Shooting, Tactics, and Combatives / Michael R. Seeklander. —1st ed.
ISBN-13: 978-1537272948
ISBN-10: 1537272942

Contents

The Low Light Fight – Shooting, Tactics, Combatives 1

Low Light Principles – The Keys to Low Light Fighting 7

Gear Talk – Selecting the Proper Low Light Tools to Win the Fight.....................................21

Shooting And Combatives – Dealing With The Threat At 1-3 Yards 29

Light Search And Engage Techniques – Finding And Adressing The Threat At 3+ Yards.............37

Room Search and Movement – Key Tactics In Your Low Light Plan 55

Low Light Training Drills – Dry Fire And Live Fire Skill Development................................61

Bonus: Defensive Rifle - Setting Up For Low Light 77

Conclusion: Action Steps..84

Dedicated to the men and women of Law Enforcement, the keepers of the peace during the dark hours when most of us sleep.

I will train my mind daily.
I will train my body daily.
I will hone my skills daily.

CHAPTER 1

Low Light Principles – The Keys to Low Light Fighting

Figure 1 If your low light position or technique does not allow you to defend your head, it has failed you!

Introduction

This is going to be a completely different angle on the low light solution, so get ready to master some effective techniques for dealing with low light situations.

One of the things that you're going to find in many books and videos that are on the market today—and some that are very high quality—is that often times their focal point is only on the shooting solution: How do I get the handgun on threat, and what flashlight technique do I use?

The reality is, if you're searching your home or a dark parking lot and you're having to integrate a handheld light and a handgun, or use a weapon-mounted light on a handgun, there are all kinds of different skill sets you need to be aware of that are separate from shooting. From how to you open the door, how to defend your head against a strike if someone is two or three feet away, or how to throw a counterstrike with a flashlight if the confines and quarters are too close for you to use your handgun. You will want to know how to shoot from different positions, whether from a retracted position or from an extended position.

Because I discuss these other aspects of the low light solution, this approach is going to be completely different.

One more thing: if I was teaching this to you as a competitive shooter, for instance how to manage your flashlight in an IDPA stage, it would be completely different in context and technique from what I am going to teach you in this defensive application. Understand very clearly that this is for integration of the flashlight and the handgun as well as the rifle in a low light environment to increase your survivability and win in a low light environment.

Since this book also contains training drills formatted to help you practice your skills, I consider it a "training program." Thank you for choosing this book! Now, let's get down to business. Let's talk about the principles that your low light system must have in it.

First of all, your flashlight technique *must* allow you to defend your head. That defense could be against a punch, or it could be against someone throwing a hammer at you that they stole out of your garage.

Your flashlight technique must be very diverse and give you the ability to protect your head, shoot, and should also allow you to throw a strike seamlessly as part of your low light plan. By this, I mean an instinctive, very fast strike to disrupt the threat in some way to allow you to move on to your next action. Remember, that strike may need to be thrown before you can shoot your handgun.

Low Light Shooting Statistics

So before we jump into principles and techniques, it is important to recognize and admit that while the low light skill is a critical one to have, sometimes its importance is overstated. Well-known trainer Tom Givens recently wrote an article summing up what he has learned from numerous shootings his students have been involved in over the years, and the data shows that we might not know as much about what is likely to happen as we think we do. A bit about Tom's data:

"Over the past 20 or so years 64 students of mine that I know about have been involved in defensive gunplay against criminals. These are the ones that I know of, who have reported back to the school or that I learned of through law enforcement contacts. Of those 64 incidents the record is 61 wins/zero losses/3 forfeits. Of the 61 students who were armed at the time of their encounter they all won and only three were injured. We have, unfortunately, had three students that I know of who lost their encounter and died. All three were killed in separate street robberies and all three were unarmed at the time of the incident, hence the term "forfeit". It's hard to win a gunfight if you did not bring your gun! Since 61 out of 61 students who were armed won their fights we must be doing something right."

Tom goes on to analyze and point out key facts that he has learned from these shootings, and specifically related to shooting in low light, this is what he summarizes:

"No student has used nor felt the need for a flashlight in any of our shootings. This is another topic in which there is a lot of misunderstanding among the shooting population.

There is an often-quoted statistic that says 80% of pistol fights occur in the dark. This is nonsense. A more accurate statement would be that 80% of pistol fights occur during the hours of darkness. For statistical purposes the hours of darkness are from 6 PM until 6 AM. Obviously in much of the country it is not dark during that entire period. Secondly, criminal encounters do not occur in a vacuum. There is no more reason for a Bad Guy to be in the dark than there is for you to be in the dark. Just because it's 3 AM on the Stop 'n Rob parking lot does not mean it's dark. In fact with modern commercial lighting I have actually seen my sights more clearly late at night on one of these parking lots than in the afternoon on an overcast day. Law enforcement officers often have to go into very dark places to search out hiding suspects. Again, it is matter of context. That is completely different than a thug approaching you on a lighted parking lot at night."

So what does that mean to you? It simply means that if you are reading this book and have not developed your basic handgun skills, and are wishing to focus on low light shooting, I suggest you prioritize and refine your fundamental skills first. Tom's training priorities are as follows, of which I strongly agree:

"Fast, efficient, reliable presentation of the handgun from concealment

The ability to accurately place several quick shots into an anatomically important area of the threat at a distance of 3 to 5 yards

The ability to place an anatomically important hit in a reasonable amount of time beyond 7 yards out to at least 25 yards

The ability to reload the handgun quickly and efficiently, especially if it holds less than 10 rounds

The ability to rapidly move off the line force (sidestep) without hindering the presentation of the pistol from concealment."

Other skills such as malfunction remedies; alternate shooting positions, such as kneeling; the use of cover; and flashlight assisted shooting techniques could be useful skills once mastery of the basic skills listed above has been accomplished. Early in your training I would prefer to see all effort directed toward competency in the core skills that I listed. I think the best approach is to model our training to match what we see occurring over and over again in the field, rather than hope what happens in the real world mirrors what we like to do on the range."

The bottom line is that while I really want you to develop the skills I have written about in this book, it would be gimmicky and dishonest if I did not point out what might even be more important. Additionally, if I really had to prioritize low light skills I would probably have you focus more on the defensive and combative aspects of using a flashlight to strike with, defend with and search with *effectively* as more important than the ability to build a good shooting position. I can think of dozens of times the average homeowner or other person may have to search, defend, or strike with a light before they might ever have to shoot with it.

That said, the way you prioritize your training should also depend on who you are and what you do. If you are a police officer working the night shift you are significantly more likely to be using your low light skills than the average civilian. As a young police officer I rarely had a night shift end without searching a building or warehouse with my flashlight after an alarm call or report of suspicious character on the premises.

I'll close with this…if you can't quickly and accurately draw and engage a threat at five yards from your carry holster, put this book down and hit the range during daylight conditions first. The low-light skill while a critical one is secondary to having the basic ability to manipulate and shoot your handgun well. Remember that in all of your training, prioritize and execute. Once you have developed a solid level of skill though, the beginning your training with the addition of low light manipulation and shooting is a must, for if you end up needing that particular skillset, things have gotten a bit edgy.

Basic Flashlight Technique - Separated or Integrated?

Now that we have talked about the statistics, let's talk about a key distinction in terms of flashlight technique I teach that may contradict what you have been taught. When you look at the predominance of shooting techniques that are taught for use with a separate flashlight (rather than a weapon-mounted light) there are two categories you're going to find.

1. *Separated—Where the handheld flashlight and gun are separate, able to do whichever technique you choose (the eye index technique, which is my personal favorite, the FBI technique, or the chin index technique).*
2. *Integrated—Where the flashlight and your hands are integrated together in some way shape or form (often called a two-handed technique).*

I will tell you this right away: generally there is one technique that will work best for you in 98% of the situations that you're going to be in, and I believe that is the separated techniques we'll spend most of our time discussing. There are

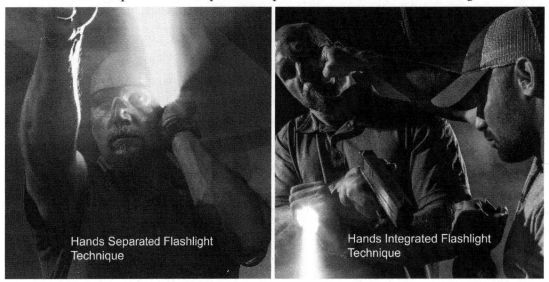

Hands Separated Flashlight Technique

Hands Integrated Flashlight Technique

Figure 2 The picture demonstrates exactly why the majority of the time I recommend using a separated hand flashlight technique. If the hands are tied together, it makes it very hard to react fast.

other techniques that we will also talk about and that I will teach you for use in that other 2%, but generally speaking I want to give you one thing that will work nearly all the time—the separated or "one hand" technique I use and teach the most.

Weapon Mounted Lights

Before I even talk about flashlight selection and use, I would be remiss if I did not mention the huge advantage that weapon mounted lights offer. The very best tool I could recommend on your home defense handgun is a weapon-mounted light with a pressure-activated switch on the handgun grip like the Streamlight TLR 2G or something similar. This solves the problem all together as far as technique is concerned. Some have an issue with a weapon mounted light (WML) and argue that they have to point the gun in a direction where someone innocent might be. My take is to keep things simple, ensure my finger is indexed along the slide and off the trigger, but there are some that prefer to search with a handheld light while they are armed with a WML and use the light to search where they need to. If you are searching with a handheld light and weapon you will be pointing the muzzle all over the place anyway, so there is no way to avoid this. The point? Use a weapon mounted light if possible.

We'll talk more about WML's in future chapters.

Low Light System

So before we get into gear and technique, I want to remind you what our low light "system" must allow us to do. It must allow us to:

1. *Defend (our head) against a physical assault (before shooting is warranted) very quickly and with little risk of pointing the muzzle at our flashlight hand.*
2. *Strike and disrupt someone without losing our weapon or light.*
3. *Search dark areas with our light in a flexible manner without having to constantly move the gun around.*
4. *Identify those that we find, preferable without having to point the gun directly at them.*
5. *Use the light as a disruption tool to give us time to make a response decision.*
6. *Identify and Engage with our handgun quickly and accurately if appropriate.*
   a. *At contact distance.*
   b. *At non-contact distances.*

Notice the order of the goals. It did not start with shooting goals, instead it started with the ones that might be more important in a environment that offers low light and a combination of both friendly's and threats. Let's get some of the common misconceptions out of the way up front. Most of these come from statements I have gotten from students or seen on the Internet.

"If someone is in my house, I'm shooting them. I have night sights on my gun I don't need to identify, and damn sure am not going to give any verbal commands before shooting. I live alone so no one will ever be in my house. My rule is shoot first and ask questions later....."

Come on folks, most of us are faced with the possibility that a drunk friend might drop in uninvited, teenage son might sneak back in late at night, or even a stupid college student forcing their way into what they thought was their dorm room. The point is that there will always be a need to identify before you use lethal force. A good low light system will give you the ability to win in those situations.

"Never use a technique where the light is close to your body. The bad guy will just shoot at the light. Hold it way out to your side and use it like that."

Okay, let's think about this for a second. The superiority of the light in most cases comes from the fact that it allows you to both blind the threat and use it's beam to make a fast decision to shoot. Try that while holding the gun away from you body, it's awkward and difficult at best. Additionally, see if the beam illuminates your sights in that position, which it won't very well. Lastly, consider this…if you are afraid of the person shooting at your light, have you considered if you are shooting at them with the muzzle flash and noise of your gun that they might have a clue where you are anyway?! Now my point is not that there will never come a time when placing the light away from your body would be prudent, but in most cases that technique falls apart or just doesn't work for the environment you are in.

An Evaluation of Technique

So let's analyze potential techniques in our system in a logical manner that will allow you to select the best one for you. While there are numerous handheld techniques out there, this section will cover the few that will allow for a small handheld light to be used since that is what you are likely to be carrying in your pocket unless you are in Law Enforcement (in which case…get a weapon mounted light!). <u>Also, I am not saying any particular technique is bad.</u> I strongly prefer a modification of the old neck index technique that I call the "eye index," but I also use two other techniques in varying circumstances. I very much respect the developers of other techniques (mostly two-handed integrated) and what they have

THE LOW LIGHT FIGHT – SHOOTING, FIGHTING, TACTICS • 15

done for low light shooting, but believe two-handed integrated techniques have many faults.

In one particular circumstance I use and recommend the Harries technique as an option (when working around cover and the threat is at a know distance), and I wholeheartedly use the Rogers flashlight gripping technique…. but just not when searching for live people in a room. I use it when competing in the sport of IDPA!

The table below breaks down some commonly found techniques and weighs them against the key requirements for our low light system to work.

Key requirements met (yes or no)			
Flashlight Technique	One handed Eye-Index	Harries	Rogers
1. Defend (our head) against a physical assault (before shooting is warranted) very quickly and with little risk of pointing the muzzle at our flashlight hand.	Yes	No	No
2. Strike and disrupt someone without losing our weapon or light.	Yes	Yes	No
3. Search dark areas with our light in a flexible manner without having to constantly move the gun around.	Yes	No	No
4. Identify those that we find, preferable without having to point the gun directly at them.	Yes	No	No
5. Use the light as a disruption tool to give us time to make a response decision.	Yes	Yes	Yes
6. Identify and Engage with our handgun quickly and accurately if appropriate. • At contact distance. • At non-contact distances.	Yes Yes	No Yes	No Yes

So if you look at the table you might notice one particular technique is the most flexible when applied to a variety of requirements. That is exactly the conclusion I came to when looking at the best technique for me, and it started with me thinking about flashlight techniques in a much broader perspective than just stable shooting platforms. If you are buying what I selling, you are going to want to know how to properly use the Eye Index technique, so let's break down some of the key principles of the technique, and I will teach you specifically how to use it in a future chapter. Here are some of it's advantages.

- *Gun Position: First, the gun position is variable, but generally speaking I like to keep my gun close to my body for retention purposes. Remember, due to the lights being off it is more likely I am going to literally run into someone at close range.*
- *Light Use: Since the gun and light are unattached and you are not trying to force your hands together in a difficult shooting position, use the light, as you need it. It can be moved independently to search rooms, the crack of a doorframe, behind a couch, etc. I try to keep the light pretty close to my head in case I have to use it to strike, shoot, or defend against a punch with it, but move the beam around as I need to.*
- **Shooting Position:** *To shoot with the light, simply index it along your temple even with your eye while activating the light with your thumb. The flat part of your knuckles should ride against the flat portion of your temple. If the light position is high enough the beam will illuminate the sights clearly and the threat, and there will not be a shadow cast in the area you are looking.*

The one exception: As stated above, I am a fan of one-handed flashlight operation, but there is one exception where I will transition to a two handed Harries technique, and that is when I am pretty certain of where the threat is in terms of distance from me, and I need to utilize cover while searching to the right. My handheld grip on the light stays the same and I can seamlessly go from separated search position to the Harries technique. One thing to

Figure 3 An example of a time when I might switch to a two-handed technique for maximum use of cover, while getting the light exposure I need IF I know the room and where the threat is.

remember is that while the Harries will feel more stable, it will not increase your ability to control recoil. Keep in mind that no matter what technique you use, you have to practice it. The easiest and simplest way to get some great skill development in is simply getting a safe red gun or S.I.R.T. pistol and a handheld light and practicing movement through your own house with a "bad guy" staged somewhere in a room. Your job is to find them and deal with them without getting punched in the face!

Of course, the one thing you will learn right away…that clearing a structure in low light unassisted is a recipe for disaster in most cases! Maybe I should have just said that up front, but simply barricading and waiting for the police to arrive is simply not an option sometimes.

The Searching and Engaging Processes

When fighting in low-light, it is important to understand the difference between the search process (before the threat is located) and engage mode (once a potential threat is located). The differences:

Search Mode – Is defined as flashlight mode in which the shooter is searching for a threat. The best process is to light up the area, take a quick look, turn the light off and move to a new position if possible. Continue this process until the threat is located or the area is cleared. Whether you are searching with a weapon mounted light or handheld light, the key is

Figure 4 Notice the position of the gun while searching; it is close to the body and retracted. This position allow me to protect the gun from a grab, defend my head, strike, or even shoot from that same retracted position if I am in a close quarters situation.

to keep the light/gun in positions where they can be used effectively and quickly. When I am searching with a weapon mounted light, I keep the gun in the "high ready" area, and move the light beam as necessary to see what I am searching. If using a handheld light, I focus on keeping the gun retracted in a protected close quarters position and have the light held up high so I can do any of the following quickly: defend my head, strike with the flashlight, and build a one-handed shooting position (eye index technique covered later in this book).

Figure 5 What do you see? Nothing! That is exactly what I want you to see when I go into engage mode, the light is blinding and your reaction time diminished. Don't believe me, test it!

Engage/Command Mode - The flashlight mode in which the shooter is either communicating with or engaging a threat. Illuminate the threat and shine the focused portion of the beam directly in the eyes. This will give several seconds of decision-making time as the light blinds the individual. If the person is a threat and shooting is warranted, engage while keeping the light turned on until there is no longer a threat.

Use the light to assess and scan after the shooting ends. In some cases where there are believed to be multiple threats, it consider turning the light off after the threat has been neutralized, so the shooter can move to a different position under the cover of darkness.

Question: Won't the bad guy simply be able to shoot at the light and hit me? Good question, but the answer requires more than just a yes or no. The bottom line is that the goal is to disrupt the person you are locating as much as possible in the first few seconds you find them. A blinding light in their eyes does just this. If they are armed and wishing to hurt you, it is possible they may shoot at your light, but think about this. During your search process don't you think they already would have known where you were? Try this, wait until your home is dark tonight and have a loved one take a bright flashlight and begin the search process. Place yourself somewhere else in the house. The bottom line is that in a dark area, the second you illuminate a light, the other person is going to know where you are, roughly. The only thing you can do about that is follow good search procedures (mentioned above), and good tactics (use of cover, etc.) until you have visually located the person, at which time using the light to disrupt the person until you have made your decision to shoot and then building that shooting position as fast as you can is your best bet.

Closing Thoughts

I've introduced you to some statistics, discussed the search and engage process and also give you a detailed breakdown or how I evaluate technique. Use those recommendations to figure out what might work best for you. In future chapters I will break down my preferred low light shooting technique in details and give you drills to practice it.

However, before we get into the specifics of techniques, first let's talk about having the right gear.

CHAPTER 2

Gear Talk – Selecting the Proper Low Light Tools to Win the Fight

Let's talk gear. When you're shopping for lowlight gear—flashlights, weapon-mounted lights, light/laser combinations—there are literally hundreds of pieces of gear out there that you could buy. This section is developed so that you can feel confident that you understand the principles behind how to choose your lowlight gear. I have used many of the top brands, and most are great pieces of gear. I believe that some specific features are very important and will advise you to look for these over the importance of a brand.

Night Sights

Let's talk about the gun first—specifically, the sights.

Here's a question for you: In a lowlight environment, do you need to have night sights on a handgun?

My answer may surprise you: "Not necessarily." That may surprise you, because you're going to see night sights on many handguns, such as all duty handguns for law enforcement and all "serious" carry guns.

So what are night sights? Night sights are simply gun sights that have some sort of radioactive component inside of them that allows them to glow-in-the-dark without having to be exposed to natural sunlight to "charge up."

Figure 6 Notice that in this picture, it is dark enough to see the night sights, but too dark to see identify or tell what the threat is doing without a flashlight.

Black gun sights or standard white sights are harder to see in dark conditions. So why would I say "maybe" to whether or not you need night sights? The reason is that when you're in dark conditions in a room or in a parking lot that are dark enough that your night sights begin to glow, you in fact most likely need an additional light source to identify a threat anyway.

If you have night sights, you are going to find a "straight 8" configuration, or a three dot configuration. Either one is fine as long as they are high quality, luminescent at all hours and not just reliant on taking on the ambient light around them to "charge up." Additionally they should allow you to accomplish all the other requirements of using a defensive handgun, such as one hand manipulation and other techniques I teach in my other courses.

Figure 7 TRUGLO Fiber optic/Tritium night sights

The bottom line is that you if have night sights, great! But if you don't ave night sights on your carry handgun or home defense handgun, that's okay. The reality is that most of you are more likely to get into a fight with your handgun during daylight or lighted conditions that would be better served by a bright, easy to see fiber optic sight rather than standard tritium night sights. My preference is to have a fiber optic front sight, which picks up light and makes the sight very visable and easy to see. There are companies on the market that make sights that are a combination of fiber optic *and* tritium so you get the best of both worlds, TRUGLO being the one that is most common in my classes.

Weapon-Mounted Lights

Weapon-moutned lights are those that are mounted to the firearm in a semi-permanent manner, usually on the light rails that are integral with most modern handguns. Weapon-mounted lights use technology that has become so advanced that if you have a handgun with a rail system and *do not* have a weapon-mounted light, you're missing out. Instead of discussing specific brands, however, I want you to understand a few principles about weapon-mounted lights—mainly the activation system.

With weapon-mounted lights, you're going to find that often times there are two different methods of activation. One popular system is a trigger guard or front grip activation system. Basically, when you grab a handgun equipped with the system and squeeze it, it activates the light.

Another type of activation system or switch is activated with the thumb of the non-shooting hand or trigger finger of the shooting hand. Typically these switches have a temporary on/off funtion as well as a full time on method of operation. You will find these switches in the form of a button on the side of the weapon-mounted light or lever device or something similar. While some light companies have an integrated switch that activates with a holster, you have to use their holster to make it work. With most of these lights, you must turn the button on or off to use the light system. Whenever you get the button, the light comes on, and whenever you hit it again, the light goes off.

I strongly prefer something with a trigger guard activation pressure switch. A switch like this operates seamlessley with one or two hands and activates as soon as you grip the handgun. The alternative is to have to constantly push a swtich with your thumb or index finger when you wish to activate the light.

In my training classes, I have lots of students show up with a weapon mounted light and no grip activation switch. I ask them how they plan to operate the light and they show me how they use the thumb to activate it. The problem is that when take one of their hands off the gun (simulating a occupied or injured hand), they have a hard time activating the light, or have to use their trigger finger. Imagine trying to activate a light switch with your index finger under the stress and time constraints of an armed threat facing you where seconds count. Would you want to grip and extend your handgun like normal allowing you to shoot immediately, or have to mess with your light switch? I think the answer is obvious.

The significant advantage of a weapon-mounted light or a light/laser combination with a grip switch is that you can have the handgun in position, without the illumination on. By simply gripping the handgun firmly, the light automatically comes on as you bring it into position. That is why I strongly recommend a light system with a integrated grip switch.

Figure 8 If you have a weapon mounted light; it is absolutely critical to have a grip mounted pressure switch to activate it.

Avoid any system that requires two hands to use. Some are designed to be activated with the thumb of the offhand, but the problem is you may not always be able to use a two-handed grip. If you have a switch that requires a special movement to activate, it may be very difficult to do so under a stressful situation.

At all costs, you must avoid any system that requires two hands to operate! You want a weapon-mounted light system that is easy to use.

If you get a weapon-mounted light, follow these two recommendations:

- *Select a weapon-mounted light with grip activation or integrated switch. If you do decide to get one with a button or already have it, make sure the button device is closely integrated and it's easy for you to place your trigger finger on it no matter which hand you're shooting with. Practice with it relentlessly!*
- *Try to find one that is a light/laser combination. The light/laser combination gives you visual feedback from the light itself, but it also puts a laser on the threat. Under stress, if you have poor vision, or if you have difficulty focusing on the sights under stress, that laser on the threat—whether it's green or red—is going to give you additional benefit over the light alone. The Streamlight TLR series is one of my favorite, and I have also used the Crimson Trace Lightguard. The Lightguard is a light only, but the company also makes a light/laser combination (the LL-801, which I have not testd).*
- *Don't buy cheap! Too many times cheap equiptment fails, and in this case it is your life you are playing with. Buy cheap coffee and beer if you must, but invest your money into the best equiptment you can get.*

Figure 9 The LL-801 , a light and laser combination with instinctive activation switch. Photo credit Crimson Trace (www.crimsontrace.com)

Again, with the technological advances today, if you do not have a weapon-mounted light, you are really missing out. Many holsters are now designed to accommodate these lights, and I believe there is nothing better for lowlight situations than having a handgun with a weapon-mounted light.

Handheld Lights

Now let's talk about handheld lights. The questions I get asked at this point in the course is, if you have a weapon-mounted light why do you need a handheld light?

Simply put, not all handguns—especially subcompacts—have a rail system to mount a weapon-mounted light. Early weapon-mounted lights all required rail systems to mount to the handgun, but now some manufacturers have systems that can be attached to the trigger guard of the handgun, which is great. But the bottom line is that you if you are carrying a very small handgun, you may not be able to mount a light to it.

Also, there are some techniques I will be teaching in this course that require a handheld light to perform, such as striking with the light, and keep in mind you may utilize your handheld light many times before ever having to draw your handgun.

Handheld lights must be able to meet certain requirements:

- *Have a thumb-activation system or button—In order to use a technique I called the "ice pick grip," you must be able to activate the light with your thumb.*

- *Sufficient illumination (but not too much)—Most modern handheld tactical lights have significant illumination. Over 100 lumens is common, which is more than enough light in a flashlight. When they first began to come out, some had less than this amount, 60-80 lumens is probably the lowest amount required. Surprisingly, too much illumination can actually be a problem. With extremely bright lights, you can run into a problem if you are in a room with white walls—the light can backwash right into your face and blind you! Some lights have become so advanced and powerful that they may not be great for inside use.*

- *Temporary and permanent activation options—You want to be able to turn the light on temporarily so that it's available only when required and while your thumb is on activation switch. But you also want to be able to activate the light and have it remain on when your thumb is no longer on the switch. As with some advanced weapon-mounted lights, many handheld tactical lights have programmable functions for strobe, dimmer settings, or other features. Some lights I have used have a separate switch for the strobe feature, which I like, but I rarely use the strobe feature when searching or illuminating a threat. A light that offers a definitive switch that is easy to operate and strobe with is fine, but I prefer to keep things as simple as possible. However, with a handheld light with a separate switch for the strobe feature, it can be a very disruptive technique! Imagine being in a dark room and then suddenly having 100 lumens or more flashing in your eyes! After all, one of the benefits of a tactical light is being able to temporarily blind a person for two or three seconds while choosing a course of action.*

- *A proper bezel—The theory behind having a sharpened (not as sharp as a knife but possibly serrated) bezel is that you can more effectively use the light to strike with. I'm a proponent of this feature, and while this feature can also be used to break out a window, it's very difficult to do so and the greater value is being able to use the light to strike with.*

- **Big enough to strike with**—*A larger light may have the benefit of more illumination or a wider beam. A larger light may also be easier to hold on to, may have a wider beam, and can be used to strike more effectively. If you need to defend yourself or strike, you want the light to extend pass the little finger in your closed hand, with you still able to activate the switch with your thumb.*

- **An LED bulb**—*Older technology used incandescent bulbs, and the downside to this was that incandescent flashlight bulbs could be fragile. If you use the light to strike with, or if you were to drop your light on a hard surface, the incandescent filament could break and your light would go out! Modern LED lights are much stronger, last longer, and require less energy to operate. They are also extremely bright! Most manufacturers have moved over to LED lights, and many older tactical lights have LED conversion kits available.*

Now that we've talked about gear, let's get on to technique. Lowlight situations involve more than having the right gear; you must learn how to run your gear properly in a lowlight situation. So let's move on to how to use your lowlight gear to defend, strike, disrupt or shoot at close range.

Figure 10 The Streamlight Protac 2L (longer version) is a great example of a handheld light that has all of the features you need on a defensive light. (photo credit Streamlight)

CHAPTER 3

Shooting And Combatives – Dealing With The Threat At 1-3 Yards

In this section we are going to cover the combative element of low light techniques. Many of these techniques will involve striking, which I cover more in depth in other programs. For example, stance, generating power, how to use your hips, balance, head position in relation to your body, etc. are all very important in proper striking in any lighting condition. If you have not checked out my program on combatives, I recommend doing that for more tips on striking. This particular section will focus on striking using the flashlight in our hands.

Positions – Where To Have The Gun

I want to point out to you that when practicing my combatives, you want to develop instinctive habits that you follow each and every time. For example, when I'm searching with my light in different rooms, I use two basic handgun positoins that I would like to define:

1. *Close Quarters High Ready Postion (one-handed because the light is in the other hand)*
2. *Extreme Close Quarters Retracted Position (one-handed because the light is in the other hand)*

The key is that during my standard room movement/search I keep the gun pulled back near my body (see the picture) to protect it and be able to transition to an extended shooting position very quickly.

When I get really close to a corner, or in a doorway beyond which there could be an unknown threat I retract the handgun even further to protect it from the possiblity of a gun grab. I also practice transitioning between those two positoins quickly as well as extending the gun into a full shooting positions so I have the skill to use the technique I need at the time. One thing I always like to consider with any handgun position is if I can shoot from it, and fight from it (combatives). If the answer is yes, then the positoin is good. With both of these positoins (high ready and retracted) you can both shoot and strike along with keeping the gun out of the reach of your attacker.

In these combatives, you will be shooting from a very compressed and retracted position or moving from that position to a standard one-hand extended firing position.

Figure 11 This is an example of using a protected position (cage) and a downward angle shot. Imagine having a light in the hand protecting the head.

There are a couple things that will stand out to you about the retracted position. First, the muzzle is below a horizontal angle and pointed slightly downward. This is important because your offhand, which is holding the light, is at shoulder level so that you can strike, parry, or do other actions. You want to keep the handgun pointed below the level of your off hand to avoid shooting yourself. While aiming low like this may not get great center of mass hits that are most effective, I can live with that because I want to have the ability to strike or defend with my off hand and flashlight while minimizing the chance that I may injure myself. Also, your threat may have innocent noncombatants behind him, and shots to the abdomen or pelvic area will drop him or immobilize him and have less chance of traveling through his body and hitting someone else.

Caging – How To Protect The Head

The entire purpose of "caging" is to protect the head from the impact of a strike, and more specifically to keep yourself from getting knocked out or down to the ground. From your position with the handgun retracted, practice caging up or covering your head and throwing a strike. If an attacker tries to strike you, you must protect your head. Without your handgun, you could use both arms to "cage," which I teach in detail in another course. If you have a handgun in your primary hand, obviously you cannot use that arm as part of your cage.

We will be working our strikes from two different cage positions: the high single-handed cage position with your arm back over your head or the low single-handed cage with your arm extended out to cover your face. With the high sign-handed cage, you bring your arm up over your head, covering the side and top of your head. In the low single-handed cage with the arm extended to cover your face, your arm and forearm are in a position to protect the majority of the front of your head, but your eyes are just below your arm. By looking down from this position, you want to still see the lower parts of your opponent. From either position, activating the light will generally provide enough light in a room for you to see your opponent.

Figure 12 This picture shows the cage position in use (actually a half-cage). The next obvious step would be to either strike off the position or potentially shoot.

From either cage position, high or low, you can come out to strike your opponent with a hammer handed blow. With either cage, the strike will typically from above his head. Above your eyes, your field of vision is somewhat limited, so when something comes down from above, you may not see it quite as clearly, especially in a lowlight situation.

Practice forming the cage with your arm covering your head, either low or high, and then bringing your fist down from above to strike with a hammer blow at the head of your practice threat. You want to have your flashlight activated as you strike. If you can strike your threat and illuminate at the same time, getting the light in his eyes, it may prevent him from seeing the strike coming, and this is a good thing for you.

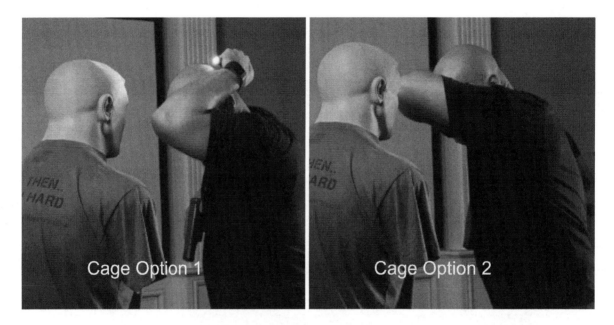

Figure 13 Either half-cage option here is viable, the key is to get the non-shooting hand into a position to defend the head and neck as quickly as possible, and practice striking from these cage positions.

When caging with option 2, with your arm covering your face, your strike will come from the side, changing the angle of the strike.

The third thing to practice is a circumstance when you are searching a room for threats when the threat pops up surprisingly. Practice quickly retracting the handgun while simultaneously striking quickly with the light, driving the light quickly into his eyes and face while activating the light.

It's important to return to a cage position directly after striking in order to protect your head and keep your light source and arm out of range for him to grapple. Never put your fist and light directly in front of your face in case he strikes and knocks the flashlight into your own face.

Striking

Striking with your flashlight is a very simple. I want to strike with what I call a hammer strike, versus a palm strike or knuckle strike. The hammer strike

Figure 14 Keep in mind that in a dynamic, low light fight, utilizing your weapon to strike might be a viable solution. Rule out nothing as a possibility.

uses your fist (and flashlight) like the head of a hammer. When you practice this, do so easy initially, with your flashlight in hand, in order to get a feel for what it's actually like to strike with your flashlight. Some flashlights may have a bezel area around the thumb switch, and when you strike hard with your flashlight you will feel that area with your thumb. When you strike hard with your flashlight, you'll get a good feel for whether or not your particular flashlight is a good choice for the combative techniques.

Practice going from recognizing the threat is there, activating your light, throwing a strike, and then caging up. You could throw two quick strikes if you have the opening, focusing on throwing each strike out there as aggressively as possible and then going to your next best position while keeping your firearm retracted. Another technique to drill is to strike first, cage, and then shoot.

Remember to keep your feet at least shoulder width apart so that you can generate plenty of torque no matter how you're striking. The idea is to disrupt your threat so that you can make a decision about what you're going to do— continue to strike, or strike, cage up, and then shoot. Either way, practice seamlessly combining the combatives of strike, cage, and shoot from a retracted position.

As you practice your combatives, you may want to add movement to the element to step out of line. In a dark room, and especially if blinded, an attacker will expect you to be where you *were*, so you want to step to your right or left quickly after striking to take you out of line and away from where your attacker saw you last.

Figure 15 To defend is one thing, but to attacking is the key. After you protect your head bring the fight to your attacker to keep them off balance.

Closing Thoughts on Combatives

In summary, when you're thinking about lowlight and you are searching the house where you suspect there may be someone in that environment hiding from you, more than likely you are going to end up at contact distance with them. You must have your contact distance combatives practiced so that they come instinctively. If your lowlight technique does not offer a combative solution to strike, protect your head, and then build a shooting position from which you can shoot from, it will fail you when the stress levels are high. Practice until your techniques are second nature.

CHAPTER 4

Light Search And Engage Techniques – Finding And Addressing The Threat At 3+ Yards

Weapon Mounted Light Techniques

After you understand some of the key principles of the low light environment, it's time to work on using your weapon-mounted light. In the gear section, I was very specific about the selection of a weapon-mounted light and the key detail that you want to try to select a weapon-mounted light with a grip activation system. The key feature to any weapon-mounted light is being able to activate it *without* having to use your fingers, thumb, or a second hand to activate the light.

My favorite is grip pressure activation, which allows me to shoot with either hand or a two-handed grip simply by squeezing the grip. Remember, you do not want any kind of light that requires two hands to operate because you may need that second hand to scoop up a child, protect yourself, or deliver a strike.

Muzzle Control With A Weapon Mounted Light

I have heard some naysayers who say that the downside to a weapon-mounted light is that whenever you are searching in a particular direction, the muzzle is pointing that way too. While I understand this perspective, I firmly believe that the weapon-mounted light is a superior tool for lowlight situations. A significant percentage of law enforcement agencies in the U.S. have weapon-mounted lights on their duty guns—because they are effective and allow them to shoot the handgun very quickly without having to manipulate a light with the other hand (if they have a grip actived pressure switch – discussed in a previous chapter).

If you are worried about your muzzle direction while searching an area, focus should be on practicing good trigger finger discipline. You can also use search techniques that do not point the muzzle at the standard elevation. For example when searching a room, keep the gun with its weapon-mounted light close to your body and pointed slightly down and "wash" the light into the room. This will illuminate the room enough for you to see what you need to in most cases, and if you spot a potential threat you can simply angle the light to see more of what you need, which includes pointing the gun directly at the person.

Keep in mind that standard range safey rules don't apply when you are faced with a potential threat that you might need to shoot.   In this case you can always de-escalate, and I strongly recommend that you keep the gun compressed and at the high ready positon until you have made the decision to actually shoot. At that time, simply extend the gun, form your firing grip and press the trigger until the threat is no longer a threat.

When searching, remember, you do not have to point the light directly at things; the light will reflect off the floor. If I do not want to point my muzzle in potentially unsafe directions, such as my child's bedroom door, by angling the muzzle down in either a high ready two-handed position or a retracted one hand position, I can illuminate an area and let the light reflect off the floor while keeping the muzzle down and in a safer position. The light will bounce and wash off the floor, still illuminating an area. In summary:

1. *Use a compressed high ready position with light angled where you need to in order to wash light into any room.*
2. *Keep the gun compressed until you have made the decision to shoot.*
3. *When you decide to shoot, extend the gun and fire the gun in a two-handed grip just like you normally would.*

Search and Engage Mode With a Weapon Mounted Light

Remember the discussion in chapter one on searching and engaging and the differneces in those two processes.   As a reminder:

- *Search Mode—In this stage, you have not yet found a threat, do not know if there is a threat, and are ready to take action if a threat is located.*
- *Engage/Command Mode—In this stage, you are ready to engage or communicate with a potential threat. Search Mode can move to Engage Mode in literally split seconds.*

So what changes with the search and engage process with a weapon mounted light? Nothing! The concept is the same and the key is that when searching with a light attached to the gun, you may have to move the gun around more than you would if you had an independent light in the non-gun hand. My preferred position with a handgun when searching in normal or low light conditions is a position I call the high ready. The high ready is a spot where the weapon is retracted toward the chest in a two handed grip, with the muzzle parallell to the ground, and finger indexed off the trigger and outside the trigger guard. The gun should be retracted and no lower than two to three inches below your chin, which makes it easier to extend and shoot if necessary.

When you enter a room in *Search Mode*—from the high ready—you are illuminating the room, washing the room in reflected light. This is why it is so important to have an easily controlled light, because you want to briefly use the light to illuminate the room as part of your search, deactivate the light, and step out of line either to your right or your left. With a grip activated weapon mounted light, when searching I simply squeeze the grip and the light activates. If I need to illuminate the crack of a door or something else that might not be directly in line with the beam, I simple angle the gun and weapon mounted light in the direction needed.

Another option with searching with a weapon mounted light is to use a handheld light along with the weapon mounted light. This makes the light use a bit more flexible, and allows you to keep the handgun retracted along your body to prevent it from a gun grab. Honestly, I feel that using a handheld light in most cases like this detracts from the benefits of having a weapon mounted light.

One/Two handed operation of the handgun occur seamlessly while I am searching, and I flow from a high ready to the close quarters position as I enter doorways or need to negotiate an obstacle with my non-shooting hand.

Figure 16 This picture shows me transitioning to the Close Quarters position to either defend my head, or possibly negotiate a door. Notice how the non-shooting hand stays clear of the muzzle.

Figure 17 High Ready position with the weapon mounted light, my standard search position unless I am in a confined space or doorway.

Engage/Command Mode begins when as part of your search you enter the room, briefly illuminate, and realize there's a potential threat in the room. When you realize there's a threat in the room, you want to get your light in their eyes as quickly as possible. Whether you decide to pull the trigger and shoot or not, which is up to you and based on circumstances, the brilliant light directed into the threat's eyes will temporarily interfere with their vision and hopefully their decision making process. Often times, shining your bright light in their eyes will give you two or three seconds where they are disoriented and cannot see properly. They will not have the ability to act for a couple of seconds and this gives you the opportunity to determine your next course of action—to shoot, move, communicate, or strike.

Decision Time

If you decide to shoot, operating with a weapon-mounted light is simple: extend to shoot, squeeze the grip-mounted switch to activate the light, and fire your shots. One of the great things about using these tools—and why you will find a weapon-mounted light on all my home defense guns—is because it's so simple. In terms of shooting, there's nothing complicated about it: point, squeeze, shoot. The light is mounted to the gun, so if you've practiced building your standard recoil control grip with one or two hands (from my other handgun series), simply extend, illuminate, and shoot. Drill this repeatedly.

This same process works if you are fighitng from an Extreme Close Quarters (ECQ) positoin, but in this case you would be retracting the gun, and shooting (please see my book Your Defensive Handgun Training Program for more on this position).

When you are finished shooting and have addressed the threat, you can then scan the area using the same technique of depressing the muzzle downward and washing light through the room and around you to check for any additional dangers.

Ending Points on Weapon Mounted Lights

In summary, I believe the weapon-mounted light is one of the best tools out there for low light defensive techniques. Don't stress over the fact that your illumination is in the same area as where the muzzle is pointing; simply depress the barrel, illuminate the area, and let the light bounce off the floor in order to light up the rooms you can identify a threat. Make sure you always practice good trigger discipline! The fact that your muzzle direction is not as controlled as it would be in daylight on the range while shooting paper threats is *not* what you need to be worried about! You need to be worried about finding a potential threat, identifying it, and doing what it takes to keep your family safe.

A weapon mounted light is an incredible tool if you train with it. Tools without training are usless. Use a weapon mounted light if you can.

But the reality is that most of us carrying small handguns daily will not have a weapon mounted light on a handgun we carry outside of our home, and for that we need another technique. Now it's time to learn how to fight with a handheld light!

Non-Weapon Mounted Light Use

Now that you know how to use a weapon-mounted light, it's important to remember that you may not always have your weapon-mounted light available. While I have one on all of my home defense weapons, when I go out of my house, I do not have a weapon-mounted light on my carry gun.

Generally speaking, most of us who carry concealed handguns outside of our home probably don't have a weapon-mounted light on our carry guns. Also, you want to have the ability and technique to use a separate flashlight in your off hand for the situations where you do not have your weapon with its weapon-mounted light available, such as when you are carrying concealed, or if your weapon-mounted light was to malfunction for some reason. That is why it's important to drill independent use of a flashlight.

Refresher

Before we do that, however, a few more quick words on which light you choose. In the gear section I mentioned that I have a few requirements for my

Figure 18 The "icepick" grip, notice how the light is deeper in the hand leaving the thumb and index finger available for use if necessary. Light shown is a Klarus.

tactical flashlights, including a thumb switch that can be either used momentarily or permanently. I also like lights that have some sort of belt clip, are longer than the width of my fist, and have a bezel for striking.

As a quick reminder from the striking section, I prefer to hold my flashlight with what I call an "ice pick" grip, where I can manipulate the switch with my thumb and where my thumb and forefinger are free enough that I can manipulate my handgun or grab a new magazine, etc. How you hold your light is critical for the technique I am going to teach you.

The Trouble with the Chin Index

In the upcoming section am going to teach you a one-handed technique called the "Eye Index Technique" that is a modification of one I learned many years ago while I worked as a trainer at the Federal Air Marshal Academy. Back in the day, we used what is called a chin or neck index, where you brought the light right up to your chin or neck. When you illuminated the light, it would wash downrange and illuminate your threat or threat. In practicing that technique and shooting it a lot, I found that there were some things I didn't like about it:

1. *If the light is at my chin, most of the beam hits my arm and the back of my hand. Reflected off my arms in a dark environment, this wash back can have the tendency to affect my night vision or even blind me.*
2. *The chin index also projects a significant shadow downrange. If there's something downrange that I want to see clearly, the shadow of my arm and hand tends to be over the top of the threat.*
3. *Finally, in this position I also cannot see my sights clearly. Most of the illumination from my flashlight is going onto my arm, not on the sights where I need it.*

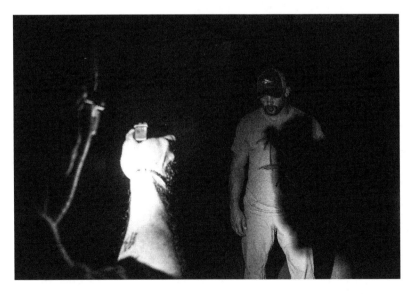

Figure 19 The problem with the chin or neck index is that the light washes off my shooting hand/arm and also shadows the target.

Introduction to the Eye Index Technique

One-Handed Eye Index Technique – As discussed above, I **strongly** recommend shooting with one-handed flashlight techniques. The main reason for my one-handed preference is that integrating both hands under stress while potentially in close range of possible threats is a recipe for disaster. Primarily because protecting the head and throwing a strike are hard and slower if the hands are tied together while using those techniques. An additional risk when things get dynamic and you attempt to separate the hands is the possibility of shooting yourself. Consider this, if you practice some of the traditional techniques that integrate the hands, you might in fact be able to shoot slightly better than with one hand at best, but you give up the all of the other advantages of having the hands independent. A solid one handed technique like the one discussed in this article leaves the support had free to search, strike and opponent, or defend the head from an attack while still being able to shoot very quickly if necessary.

The technique I teach is called the "eye index", and is my modification of the neck index I learned at the Federal Air Marshal Training Academy years ago. To perform the *eye index* place the flashlight with the activator button in the support hand with the activator button by the thumb. The flashlight should be indexed alongside the face approximately in line with the eye. If the flashlight is indexed lower, the gun will be highlighted and a shadow will be cast on the threat. The indexed flashlight is held to the face so when the head turns, the flashlight illuminates the area in front of the face. When the eye index technique is used ensure you place the flashlight in a position that allows the free use of the thumb and index finger to reload or clear a malfunctions. To do this you can simply use your index finger and thumb to manipulate your gun while retaining control of the flashlight.

One more thing about this technique, and flashlight shooting techniques in general, is that no matter what technique you use; you will be a threat as soon as you turn the flashlight on.   While the old FBI methods used to attempt to prevent this by placing the light away from the body, the technique is very hard to use effectively.   Admittedly, my eye index technique places the light in a spot that causes it to be right next to the head and some of you might think this is a horrible idea since the light will become threat.   Consider this though, no matter what technique you use to shoot with, you will have the light (and threat) around your head, or upper chest.   The second you illuminate the light you will immediately illuminate yourself and there really is no place to hide.   Instead of trying to manage the possibility of someone shooting at your light, instead focus your attention on making fast decisions and shooting if necessary.   There is no such thing as a flashlight shooting technique that will not immediately make you a threat when you turn the light on.

Figure 20 The Eye Index Technique done right. Notice the placement of the light, and consistent one-handed shooting position (the same as my daylight position).

Eye Index Specifics

What I discovered was that if I moved the light up nearer to the top of my head, I found a spot roughly even with my temple and slightly above my eye where all of the illumination goes over the top of my gun, illuminating my sights and whatever is downrange. Clearly illuminating your sights is very important for being able to aim accurately, and it's always good to get as much light as possible downrange. The eye index position lets me see who is downrange and allows me to quickly identify whether or not they are a threat. This largely eliminates shadow that is a problem with the chin index technique.

When I'm shooting from this position—the one-handed eye index position—I index the flashlight at my temple with my finger bones flat against my temple right above my eye, and I use the same one-handed position for the firearm I would normally use. (I strongly suggest you check out my course on handgun technique and refresh yourself on one-handed shooting, but by way of a quick reminder make sure you are positioned with your arm behind the gun and your body weight behind your arm.)

When you index the light to your head, keep the light next to your head as you move your head. Let's say that you thought you heard a noise, you index the light to your head, and then you realize the noise was further to your right. As you turn your head, keep the light indexed to your head, turning with the motion of your head. The light should point everywhere you look. I really like the eye index position as a shooting position but also for how easy it makes it to point the light at whatever you are looking at.

Keep in mind however, I am not gluing the light to my head the entire time, only when needed to shoot. During most of the process I am moving the light beam around where needed as I search, keeping it in an area near my head and shoulder so I can use it to shield my head, strike, or shoot if necessary.

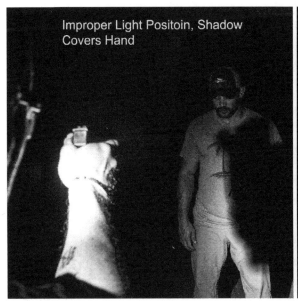
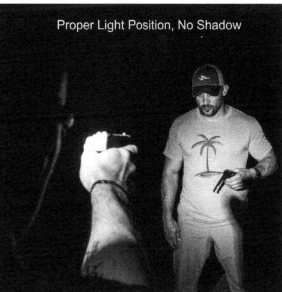

Figure 21 This picture shows the shadow effect from having the light too low, which covers up portions of the threat and/or their hands limiting your ability to make decisions.

Separate and Appropriate

It's important to note that when you're in Search Mode that you do not do so in the eye index position with the light next to your head. Instead, we want to use the gun and light separately and appropriately. Let's talk about what that means.

- *Remember, you want your gun in a controlled, retracted position, where it's close to your body and easy to hold for long periods of time. That way the weapon is in a better retention position, so if someone jumps at you, the gun is not up in front of your face and body where it could be grabbed and taken away from you. You'll have a better chance of retaining your gun in the retracted position.*

- *While you are searching, your light will vary in position in a sort of box relatively close to head level. If you are searching the edge of a wall, you will move your arm appropriately to search past the edge of the wall, up and down. You want to be able to move the light around to illuminate above and around objects. However, in general the light stays close to your head and ready for the eye index position. Though you may move the angle of the light to search, you want to be able to index the light to your temple quickly when needed. By keeping the light close, you can quickly index the light to your eye and extend the gun into a proper one-handed shooting position.*

Eye Index Drills

Indexing the light to your temple and moving from a retracted position to a shooting position is an important drill. You can use a S.I.R.T. (Shot Indicating Resetting Trigger made by Next Level Training) pistol or other training tool—do not do this with your live firearm—and your flashlight. Practice searching through your home and indexing the flashlight and gun. It can be helpful to get someone to participate with you by hiding and popping up so that you can practice indexing properly when surprised, which is again why it is important to always use proper firearm safety and not to do your drills with your live firearm. Also, you can practice stepping out of line to the right or left and issuing commands.

Remember the key details of *Search Mode* and *Engage/Communicate Mode*. When searching, you quickly illuminate, looking for threats, and then step out of line to the right or left. The idea is that your quick use of the light should allow you to identify the presence of a threat, but then you step out of line so that you are no longer standing where you were when you illuminated your light in case the threat fires where he last saw your light. If he fires, you do not want to be there! Briefly illuminate your light, look, and move.

Once you have walked into a room, illuminated, and stepped to the side, if you observed a threat, shine your light into the threat's eyes as you index the light and your weapon. Again, this buys you some time—precious seconds where the threat cannot see properly because of your bright light. You will now have a couple of seconds to make your decision about whether to engage, move again, and/or issue commands.

It's important to note that you must practice the decision-making process a when to shoot. How to issue commands safely is important because you cannot just shoot anyone who comes into your home. Perhaps you have a teenage daughter and her idiot teenage boyfriend is in your house; as much as you might like to, you can't simply shoot him automatically. Instead, you must be able to safely issue commands.

Briefly disrupting the threat will give you a few moments to make your decision and do what you need to do.

In a very small number of situations, I find that it is appropriate to put my hands together in a two-handed position, such as the two-handed technique developed by Michael Harries, the former Marine who promoted the Harries Technique, or Bill Roger's technique. These two-handed techniques are rarely used, but every once in a while there is a circumstance where you may need to use them. We will cover those next.

Two-Handed Technique

We previously discussed the one-handed eye index technique, and I also mentioned that there are very rare cases where I would recommend using a two-handed technique. In this section, we will cover the two two-handed techniques that I recommend, and I will tell you when I would recommend using them.

I want to reemphasize the importance of training so that you can effectively use a good one-handed technique where both weapon and flashlight move independently. In the environment of your home, the one-handed technique allows you to seamlessly go from search to indexing in preparation to shoot, to guard your head, to strike, to pick up a frightened child, etc., without your hands being effectively tied together. Earlier, I told you that the one-handed technique will cover 98% of the lowlight circumstances you will encounter.

Harries Technique and Bill Rogers' Technique

However, there are situations where a two-handed technique is required. There are two main two-handed techniques that I use and recommend. One was developed by Michael Harries, a former Marine who developed what we call the Harries Technique. When I was in the Federal Air Marshalls, I called this the back to back position because the backs of your hands are tied together. Lock your wrists together with your light in your offhand and your pistol in your dominant hand, and from there out the two hands operate as one.

Your grip on your flashlight is the same "ice pick" style grip I have mentioned before, which allows you to activate the light with your thumb. In addition to having the backs of your hands together, back to back, exert isometric tension between your hands— you are actually pushing your strong hand into your

Figure 22 A good example of when I might switch to the Harries technique, a threat at distance, and need to get the illumination past the wall. Recoil control is no better than shooting one handed however.

support hand and your support hand into your strong hand. By moving them together, whatever you illuminate you can also shoot.

The downside to this technique is that while it illuminates the downrange area, it does not illuminate your sights. If you don't have night sights, there will be some limitations with this technique. Also, of course your two hands are now tied together, and your offhand is not free to manipulate your environment.

The other technique is modeled after Bill Rogers' technique of holding your light between the index and second finger of your off hand and activating the light with the palm of your hand. This allows you to actually wrap around and build something very similar to your normal two-handed shooting grip. In this particular grip, the light will tend to point downward slightly, but it's the only two-handed technique that I know that offers the ability to grip the gun and control the recoil thanks to two hands. It's probably the best pure shooting technique that I know of if you're trying to hold a light. I use it extensively when competing in low light but do not prefer it for real life searching where I might have to defend my head or throw a strike. The technique requires a good deal of practice and that is especially true when you are taking your hand off the gun to manipulate it (reload, malfunction) and place it back on the gun.

The downside is that if you don't already have the flashlight set up and ready to go, it takes some time to build. For example, if you are searching with your flashlight in the ice pick grip, to use the Rogers technique, you have to switch the light between your fingers and try to re-grip your handgun. While it's doable, it's not a technique that I want to use most of the time due to the limitation on my ability to strike or defend. One last thing about that particular technique is that you need to test it during live fire shooting to make sure that you are actually controlling the gun and secondly to make sure you do not accidentally push the light against the magazine release and drop the magazine out of the gun. Needless to say, in a fight that would be bad.

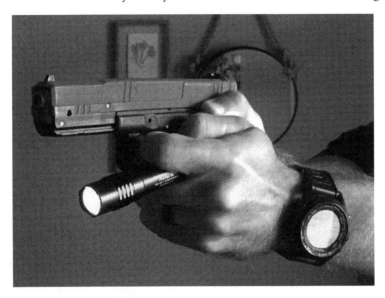

Figure 23 A variation of the technique taught by Bill Rogers is probably one of the best overall shooting techniques you will find. This one takes practice though, and has limited combatives application.

When to Go Two-Handed

When we are discussing two-handed techniques, the important thing to understand is the circumstances when you would need to use them. Why would you not simply use the eye index technique we discussed earlier? Let's say you're out in your yard, and you have a big yard. You've heard a bump in the night, and for whatever reason instead of going to your safe area and calling 911, you choose to search your yard. Or you may be in a large open space and you suspect there's a threat out there. Because of the potential threat, when you try to use your one-handed technique, you find that you're shaking like crazy because you're too amped up or frightened.

This may be a circumstance for transitioning to a two-handed technique in order to stabilize your shooting hand. If you know for a fact that you're not a very good one-handed shooter and you don't think you can get the shots off accurately, you may want to bring that second hand alongside the handgun in order to give more stability to your shooting hand.

Understand, you're not going to have a lot of effect on recoil with these techniques. The only recoil control you're going to have is the isometric tension between your hands.

The final situation where you might want to use two-handed grip and the one I find myself using is if you are searching along the wall or corner of a door attempting to use it for cover and using the eye index technique would wash too much light back up into your face. Your options are to switch to a One-handed Eye Index position with the light on the other side of your head (see pic) or switch to a two handed technique. Just remind yourself of the limitations of tieing two hands together.

Figure 24 This shows your two options when working around a door or wall and wish to use cover effectively (shown with a right handed shooter). Switch the eye-index to the other side of the head, or use a two-handed position.

The key is understanding when the one-handed technique is no longer optimal and being able to seamlessly switch from the one-handed position to a two-handed technique. Practice moving your offhand from the side of your head and bringing it up under your shooting arm and sliding it up until your hands meet. Be sure to not put your flashlight hand in front of your gun!

Final Thoughts on Technque

In the circumstances where a two-handed technique is necessary, you need to be able to seamlessly switch to it. When you practice your drills, both your dry fire drills and your live fire drills, practice switching to the two-handed technique in context. Set up a situation where your threat is further out then you would use when practicing with your one-handed technique—instead of seven yards out, do it at 14 yards out for example. Simulate the use of cover as well so that you can simulate using the two-handed technique in the context that you may actually have to use it. Be sure you have sufficiently practice these techniques so that you can use them effectively—get out on the range and use these techniques in their context.

CHAPTER 7

Room Search and Movement – Key Tactics In Your Low Light Plan

It's time to discuss how to move through a lowlight situation, searching for threats. For this section, we will be assuming you are using a one-handed technique.

First of all, retract the handgun backward in close to your side. Your flashlight will stay in an area near your head so that you can quickly index it, form a cage to protect your head, strike, or move the light in order to search around objects. Focus on moving from technique to techniques seamlessly as you practice searching through your home.

Getting Out the Door

Now to tackle a difficult subject: opening a doorknob! The key difference is that you are having to maintain your grip on your flashlight while manipulating the doorknob, and if you are holding your light properly, your index finger and your thumb should be available for opening the door or doing whatever else you need to do. With your gun in a high gun position, reach out with your off hand and use the index finger and thumb to manipulate the door. (Practice gripping the doorknob without making contact between the doorknob and the flashlight till you can do it quietly.) As soon as you begin to open the door, get your thumb back on the activation switch. Remember, you want to illuminate whatever is beyond the door the moment you open it.

As you pull the door open, step back quickly and briefly illuminate through the doorway. Search for threats, and move the light to illuminate any areas beyond the doorway. Search the edge of the wall as you move forward, and as you approach the doorway, retract the gun even further. Pass through the doorway and into the room, washing the light through the room and then as you go through each doorway and enter a new room.

Figure 25 This is how to handle a door. Notice the muzzle position (not covering hand) and also the handheld light in my hand.

As you step into a new area, practice briefly washing the light through the room and then moving, stepping out of the line of fire.

Walls are more of the same—move along the wall and angle your wrist to shine the light all around without moving it from the box near your head so that you can quickly index it if you spot a threat.

Remember, as you move into a new section, you're not leaving the light on—you're turning it on as you step into the new room, washing the room in light, deactivating the light, and then moving out of line quickly.

Build in Surprises

Set up—or better yet, have someone else set up—a threat, so that you can practice moving from searching to the eye index technique, extending the firearm into a shooting position, and taking the shot. (Again, don't forget to use all proper safety while practicing by never using a live firearm for home search drills!)

When you put the drill together with your practice weapon, your light, and a threat, you can refine your techniques so you can effectively clear your house. If you want to amp it up, get a family member to hide and practice being a threat that can leap out and surprise you. Give them the chance to throw some light strikes so you can practice defending your head and delivering strikes.

Strobing and Other Trickery

If you do any research on low-light training and techniques, it is very likely you will find much material that embraces methods of low light searching that can seem to be gimmicky. An example is a technique called "strobing," which is basically the quick flashing of a light in order to increase the disruption felt by the threat due to the effect of the eyes and brain. While there seem to be many different theory's on how strobing effects humans, I agree that a high lumen light in a strobing pattern can be quite effective in disrupting a potential threat.

The problem is that strobing also affects the user in a dark room, and the technique is often times hard to pull off consistently. For example, in years past, some instructors taught their students to quickly strobe the light be pushing the button very fast when searching different areas of a room or when encountering a threat. Then, upon finding a threat the user was supposed to activate the light and shoot using a variety of techniques they may have learned. The problem is that in a high stress environment the brain can get confused to which is which and the pattern gets screwed up.

In recent years, several light companies have developed lights that have a strobe function. Some of them are activated by a different number of pushes on the thumb activation button, for example the first push activates the

Figure 26 Klarus XTC1C light sold by Tulster.com, a great option if you wish to have a light with a separate strobe activation button.

light, second push activates a lower lumen light, and third push activates the strobe. I STRONGLY advise against such a set up, as during the search process it is very easy to mistakenly go from one beam patter to the next without meaning to. Unless your light has a secondary switch (Like the Klarus XT1C or similar), I strongly recommend selecting or programming your light to have one function. The Streamlight products I use (Protac 1 and 2L) have a feature called 10-step programming which allows the user to program whichever function they choose, and for my defensive lights I stick to one activation = one type of function. A camping light or work tool is great with a low lumen feature, but a fighting light should do one thing consistently.

Final Thoughts on Room Search and Movement

You can practice everything you need to master about low light techniques in the comfort of your own home. You'll learn a lot from moving through your home, moving beyond doorways or along walls, dealing with windows and mirrors, and all the rest of the variables in your environment that you'll need to master to use these techniques effectively.

Remember, in your home, you're on your home turf! You have home court advantage over any intruder, so know your home and how to clear it efficiently using the proper techniques and transitioning seamlessly between them as the situation dictates. Take your advantage and use it to keep you and your family safe!

CHAPTER 8

Low Light Training Drills – Dry Fire And Live Fire Skill Development

The next sections contain the dry and live fire drill sheets. These sheets will guide your training and skill development while at home (dry fire). Feel free to modify distances as appropriate.

Each Drill and technique in this book is show in full detail in a series of videos that can found:

1. *On the American Warrior Society website:* http://www.americanwarriorsociety.com
2. *On Vimeo (Full downloadable on demand series):*
   https://vimeo.com/ondemand/lowlight101

Medium Range Index and Shoot Dry Fire Drill

Purpose: To build the indexing skill of bringing the flashlight to the correct spot and coordinating that with the gun position.

Start Position: Empty gun with slide cycled (hammer cocked), with the handgun at the high/compressed ready.

Threat Type and Setup: One 1/3 size small threat (humanoid shape) set directly in front of the shooter at room distance (5-7 yards).

Prop Setup: N/A

Action(s): On the start signal, index the light and extend the handgun and fire (click) three to five times, aiming at the center of the appropriate threat. Go through a scan process (check around you and behind you) with the flashlight before administratively working the slide to prepare for the next training repetition.

Critical Points: Make sure to deliberately ride the thumb safety and wipe it off as you extend the handgun if you shoot a 1911. Strive to make the technique consistent by finding the proper index points during the process during each repetition, such as a specific flashlight position. This will ensure a consistent sight picture and flashlight use, as the eye will be aligned behind the sights consistently.

Visual Cues: Visual shift from the threat aiming area back to the front sight. Proper illumination of the sights and no shadow on the threat.

Mental Cues: Actively visualize the entire drill. Ensure you visualize the technique components (active visualization), as well as elements of a real scenario (that the threat is real).

Medium Range Draw, Index and Shoot Dry Fire Drill

Purpose: To build the indexing skill of bringing the flashlight to the correct spot and coordinating that with the gun position, from the draw.

Start Position: Empty gun with slide cycled (hammer cocked), with the handgun holstered and flashlight wherever you carry it.

Threat Type and Setup: One 1/3 size small threat (humanoid shape) set directly in front of the shooter at room distance (5-7 yards).

Prop Setup: N/A

Action(s): On the start signal, draw and index the light and handgun and fire (click) three to five times, aiming at the center of the appropriate threat. Go through a scan process (check around you and behind you) with the flashlight before administratively working the slide to prepare for the next training repetition.

Critical Points: Make sure to deliberately ride the thumb safety and wipe it off as you extend the handgun if you shoot a 1911. Strive to make the technique consistent by finding the proper index points during the process during each repetition, such as a specific flashlight position. This will ensure a consistent sight picture and flashlight use, as the eye will be aligned behind the sights consistently.

Visual Cues: Visual shift from the threat aiming area back to the front sight. Proper illumination of the sights and no shadow on the threat.

Mental Cues: Actively visualize the entire drill. Ensure you visualize the technique components (active visualization), as well as elements of a real scenario (that the threat is real).

Long Range Draw, Index and Shoot Dry Fire Drill

Purpose: To build the indexing skill of reacting to and switching to a secondary technique (Harries) for longer range shooting or a shaky platform.

Start Position: Empty gun with slide cycled (hammer cocked), with the handgun holstered and flashlight wherever you carry it.

Threat Type and Setup: One 1/3 size small threat (humanoid shape) set directly in front of the shooter at room distance (5-7 yards).

Prop Setup: N/A

Action(s):   You can start this from the Eye Index technique (as if you were already on threat and realized transitioning to a secondary technique was necessary, or from the holster). On the start signal, practice switching to the alternate technique by placing the back of the hand on the outside of the gun hand forearm and sliding the hand down the arm into the proper shooting position.   Fire (click) three to five times, aiming at the center of the appropriate threat. Go through a scan process (check around you and behind you) with the flashlight before administratively working the slide to prepare for the next training repetition.

Critical Points: Strive to make the technique consistent by finding the proper point of placement for both hands during each repetition. This will ensure a consistent sight picture and flashlight use, as the eye will be aligned behind the sights consistently.

Visual Cues: Visual shift from the threat aiming area back to the front sight. Proper illumination of the threat. Keep in mind that your sights will not be as illuminated with this technique.

Mental Cues: Actively visualize the entire drill. Ensure you visualize the technique components (active visualization), as well as elements of a real scenario (that the threat is real).

Close Range Strike, Cover, Shoot Dry Fire Drill

Purpose: To build the skill of striking with the light, and then covering the head in a proper cage position while at the same time building a close quarter shooting position to engage from.

Start Position: Empty gun with slide cycled (hammer cocked), with the handgun at the high/compressed ready.

Threat Type and Setup: Practice dummy or a full size threat (humanoid shape) set directly in front of the shooter and mounted so it can be struck (1 yards).

Prop Setup: N/A

Action(s): On the start signal, strike the threat in the appropriate spot, retract the hand to cover the head while retracting the handgun, index the proper close quarters shooting position and fire (click) three to five times. Create distance and go through a scan process (check around you and behind you) with the flashlight before administratively working the slide to prepare for the next training repetition.

Critical Points: Make sure to deliberately ride the thumb safety and wipe it off as you extend the handgun if you shoot a 1911. Pay particular attention to the cover and gun position in this drill.

Visual Cues: Keep eyes open and use ambient light to verify where the threat/threat is.

Mental Cues: Actively visualize the entire drill. Ensure you visualize the technique components (active visualization), as well as elements of a real scenario (that the threat is real).

Close Range Strike, Cover, Shoot Live Fire Drill

Purpose: To build the skill of striking with the light, and then covering the head in a proper cage position while at the same time building a close quarter shooting position to engage from.

Start Position: Note: Practice this drill dry fire first. You must have a safe range surface to perform this drill on. Start with a fully loaded gun at the high/compressed ready.

Threat Type and Setup: Practice dummy or a full size threat (humanoid shape) set directly in front of the shooter and mounted so it can be struck (1 yards).

Prop Setup: N/A

Action(s): On the start signal, strike the threat in the appropriate spot, retract the hand to cover the head while retracting the handgun, index the proper close quarters shooting position and fire three to five times. Remove the finger from the trigger guard and create distance and go through a scan process (check around you and behind you) with the flashlight before administratively working the slide to prepare for the next training repetition.

Critical Points: Make sure to deliberately ride the thumb safety and wipe it off as you extend the handgun if you shoot a 1911. Pay particular attention to the cover and gun position in this drill.

Visual Cues: Keep eyes open and use ambient light to verify where the threat/threat is.

Mental Cues: Actively visualize the entire drill. Ensure you visualize the technique components (active visualization), as well as elements of a real scenario (that the threat is real).

Live Fire Drills

This section will contain the low light live fire drills you will use in this system. As a reminder from normal light live fire: These drills are specifically designed to allow you to work through the firing cycle and improve your ability to manage three things: 1) sights (gun direction); 2) trigger; and 3) recoil control AND integrate a flashlight. If you have not worked through the standard training drills, I recommend you start there. Specifically covered:

1. *Skills trained in the live fire program*
2. *Live fire training schedule*
3. *Execution of live fire training sessions (pre, during and post session)*
4. *Live fire training drills*
5. *Live fire training phases*
6. *Procedures for performing the drills*

Skills Trained

The live-fire training module will improve your ability to shoot better and integrate smart procedures such as performing an after-action scan process. Remember, the firing cycle is the trigger, sight, and recoil management that you must master in order to shoot fast and hit your threat. You will primarily develop your manipulation skills in dry fire, so the focus will be on improving elements of the firing cycle during your live fire sessions, integrating the mental visualization techniques mentioned in the mental section, and performing correct tactics.

Generally speaking, your live fire training time is better spent if you are focusing on the concepts of improving your ability to hit the threat faster and more accurately. Always focus intently on what the handgun is doing during recoil and attempt to improve your ability to put rounds on threat faster. Remember, you will work on your manipulation skills primarily in dry fire sessions.

Low Light Training Schedule

In the normal handgun program, you will be doing one live fire session on the range each week. Once you have completed the full program I recommend you add at least one monthly night of low light training at the range (and several at home with dry fire). Pick a drill or two and focus on developing skill.

Medium Range Index and Shoot Live Fire Drill

Purpose: To build the indexing skill of bringing the flashlight to the correct spot and coordinating that with the gun position.

Start Position: Loaded gun with slide cycled (hammer cocked), with the handgun at the high/compressed ready.

Threat Type and Setup: One full size threat (preferable IDPA or humanoid shape) set directly in front of the shooter at room distance (5-7 yards).

Prop Setup: N/A

Action(s):   On the start signal, index the light and extend the handgun and fire through a progression of four (1-2-3-4). Go through a scan process (check around you and behind you) with the flashlight before beginning the next training repetition.

Critical Points: Make sure to deliberately ride the thumb safety and wipe it off as you extend the handgun if you shoot a 1911. Strive to make the technique consistent by finding the proper index points during the process during each repetition, such as a specific flashlight position. This will ensure a consistent sight picture and flashlight use, as the eye will be aligned behind the sights consistently.

Visual Cues: Visual shift from the threat aiming area back to the front sight. Proper illumination of the sights and no shadow on the threat.

Mental Cues: Actively visualize the entire drill. Ensure you visualize the technique components (active visualization), as well as elements of a real scenario (that the threat is real).

Medium Range Draw, Index and Shoot Live Fire Drill

Purpose: To build the indexing skill of bringing the flashlight to the correct spot and coordinating that with the gun position.

Start Position: Loaded gun with slide cycled (hammer cocked), with the handgun holstered and flashlight in the carry position.

Threat Type and Setup: One full size threat (preferable IDPA or humanoid shape) set directly in front of the shooter at room distance (5-7 yards).

Prop Setup: N/A

Action(s): On the start signal, index the light and extend the handgun and fire through a progression of four (1-2-3-4). Go through a scan process (check around you and behind you) with the flashlight before beginning the next training repetition.

Critical Points: Make sure to deliberately ride the thumb safety and wipe it off as you extend the handgun if you shoot a 1911. Strive to make the technique consistent by finding the proper index points during the process during each repetition, such as a specific flashlight position. This will ensure a consistent sight picture and flashlight use, as the eye will be aligned behind the sights consistently.

Visual Cues: Visual shift from the threat aiming area back to the front sight. Proper illumination of the sights and no shadow on the threat.

Mental Cues: Actively visualize the entire drill. Ensure you visualize the technique components (active visualization), as well as elements of a real scenario (that the threat is real).

Medium Range, Index and Shoot Live Fire Drill With Cover

Purpose: To build the indexing skill of bringing the flashlight to the correct spot and coordinating that with the gun position on the left and right hand side of cover.

Start Position: Loaded gun with slide cycled (hammer cocked), with the handgun holstered and flashlight in the carry position.

Threat Type and Setup: One full size threat (preferable IDPA or humanoid shape) set directly in front of the shooter at room distance (5-7 yards).

Prop Setup: One barricade or piece of cover that allows you to shoot around it with no danger of splashback.

Action(s):   On the start signal, index the light and extend the handgun and fire through a progression of four (1-2-3-4) from the left side of cover. Repeat the drill from the right hand side by alternating the light position or technique (to a two-handed technique or light on the other side of head). Go through a scan process (check around you and behind you) with the flashlight before beginning the next training repetition.

Critical Points: Make sure you build a position where the light does not wash back into your eyes and blind you. Strive to make the technique consistent by finding the proper index points during the process during each repetition, such as a specific flashlight position. This will ensure a consistent sight picture and flashlight use, as the eye will be aligned behind the sights consistently.

Visual Cues: Visual shift from the threat aiming area back to the front sight. Proper illumination of the sights and no shadow on the threat.

Mental Cues: Actively visualize the entire drill. Ensure you visualize the technique components (active visualization), as well as elements of a real scenario (that the threat is real).

Long Range Draw, Index and Shoot Live Fire Drill

Purpose: To build the indexing skill of reacting to and switching to a secondary technique (Harries) for longer range shooting or a shaky platform.

Start Position: Loaded gun with slide cycled (hammer cocked), with the handgun holstered and flashlight in the carry position.

Threat Type and Setup: One full size threat (preferable IDPA or humanoid shape) set directly in front of the shooter at room distance (5-7 yards).

Prop Setup: N/A

Action(s): You can start this from the Eye Index technique (as if you were already on threat and realized transitioning to a secondary technique was necessary, or from the holster). On the start signal, practice switching to the alternate technique by placing the back of the hand on the outside of the gun hand forearm and sliding the hand down the arm into the proper shooting position. Fire through a progression of four, aiming at the center of the appropriate threat. Go through a scan process (check around you and behind you) with the flashlight before doing the next repetition.

Critical Points: Strive to make the technique consistent by finding the proper index points during the process during each repetition, such as a specific flashlight position. This will ensure a consistent sight picture and flashlight use, as the eye will be aligned behind the sights consistently.

Visual Cues: Visual shift from the threat aiming area back to the front sight. Proper illumination of the sights and no shadow on the threat.

Mental Cues: Actively visualize the entire drill. Ensure you visualize the technique components (active visualization), as well as elements of a real scenario (that the threat is real).

Close Range Strike, Cover, Shoot Live Fire Drill

Purpose: To build the skill of striking with the light, and then covering the head in a proper cage position while at the same time building a close quarter shooting position to engage from.

Start Position: Empty gun with slide cycled (hammer cocked), with the handgun at the high/compressed ready.

Threat Type and Setup: Practice dummy or a full size threat (humanoid shape) set directly in front of the shooter and mounted so it can be struck (1 yards). ENSURE YOU HAVE A PROPER IMPACT AREA FOR THE DOWNWARD ANGLE OF THE SHOT DURING THIS DRILL.

Prop Setup: N/A

Action(s): On the start signal, strike the threat in the appropriate spot, retract the hand to cover the head while retracting the handgun, index the proper close quarters shooting position and fire through a progression of four. Create distance and go through a scan process (check around you and behind you) with the flashlight before stepping back up to the threat and preparing for the next training repetition.

Critical Points: Make sure to deliberately ride the thumb safety and wipe it off as you extend the handgun if you shoot a 1911. Pay particular attention to the cover and gun position in this drill. SAFETY is the key.

Visual Cues: Keep eyes open and use ambient light to verify where the threat/threat is.

Mental Cues: Actively visualize the entire drill. Ensure you visualize the technique components (active visualization), as well as elements of a real scenario (that the threat is real).

Advanced Skill Developing Low Light Drills

After using the above drills to train your low light skills, try a few drills from the book *Your Defensive Handgun Training Program* (www.shooting-performance.com) program that will help you develop a really high level of skill. They are all great drills to try in low light to challenge your skills. I recommend using them as bonus training drills, as well as the normal drills you might find helpful to further your low light skills, just add the flashlight or weapon mounted light.

CHAPTER 9

Bonus: Defensive Rifle - Setting Up For Low Light

You MUST positively identify any potential threat PRIOR to engaging it and that requires a light. Understanding that time is not necessarily on our side during an encounter in our home, it only makes sense to have a light permanently attached to our Defensive Rifle. This way, the light is always with the rifle and is always available for use. A weapon light should have the brightest possible light in the smallest lightweight package available, within reason. The "reason" I write it like that is because there are actually lights made today that are too bright for certain uses. Some of the lights on the market that could be mounted to a rifle today might have more than 300 lumens (and some double that!). A light this bright will almost instantly blind you in confined spaces with light colored walls. A light that that much intensity is best served on a hunting platform (if legal) or possibly on a rifle that will be exclusively used outside.

Light Selection

The Streamlight TLR-2 HL light/laser combination I have on my rifle is probably the upper end of intensity I would want to use. Streamlight advertises this light as 630 lumens and 12,000 candelas. Streamlight also makes a TLR-1 HPL (High Lumen, Long-Range Rail-Mounted tactical Light) that is advertised with 775 lumens, and an incredibly focused beam. This light this would be over-

Figure 27 The top light is the Streamlight TLR-2 HL light/laser combination I like. The bottom is the TLR-1 HPL, and great light but made for a specific purpose. Make sure you select the right light! NOTE: The rifle pictured on the bottom is upside down.

kill and a detriment if your defensive solution was your house and yard. The light is so bright and focused that it creates a blindingly bright spot when it hits a wall and this "hot spot" stays imbedded in your vision after illuminating it. I would not suggest a light this powerful. It should have a provision for momentary and permanent activation through the use of a remote pressure pad or through direct hand activation. Batteries should be of a standard size that is easily acquired at any store without special order.

Light Placement

Care must be given as to the placement of the light on the Defensive Rifle. Ensure placement of the light or the activation pressure pad is consistent with your hand placement during the shooting process. Placement should be at our near your support hand position. Switching hand positions to activate the light is inefficient. Proper placement brings efficiency to our technique and speed is a by-product of efficiency. If you have a vertical or angled foregrip on your rifle, then make sure you find a mounting solution for your light activation switch that will be consistent with either hand. I have had many students in my classes realize that their mounting solution was poor when I had them switch to the other hand and they had the light pressure switch mounted and accessible only on one side of the gun.

Note: The light position on the rifle is of critical importance. I have tried the three, nine, six and twelve o'clock positions and one thing to consider is the fact that when a light is mounted anywhere other than six o'clock, you will have problems. In the past I experimented extensively with light positions. One position I tried was the twelve o'clock position, mainly because I figured mounting a Surefire or similar light at twelve o'clock and using my thumb to activate the toggle switch was a simple solution that would allow me to skip mounting a pressure pad on the rifle. In past testing with this position, I had observed problems with the smoke from the rifle muzzle obscuring the threat. While I knew that the twelve o'clock mounting position of the light was not the best option, I had convinced myself that at the ranges I would likely operate my rifle, the smoke obscuring my vision would not be an issue. I was wrong! Even at closer ranges of ten yards, the smoke became an issue with multiple rounds fired, and with the light mounted at twelve o'clock; the smoke issue was huge, especially when using an optic (an Aimpoint C3 in this case).

At more than fifty yards, the smoke completely covered the threats and kept me from shooting for a second or so until it cleared enough for me to see the next threat. After I mounted the light at the six o'clock position, the smoke problems became almost none existent due to the fact that the light was no longer illuminating the smoke in front of my scope. As stated before, the three and nine o'clock positions are not recommended because of the increase in splash back that the shooter will get from those positions while working around cover. See the photo below for exactly how and where I mounted my light.

The picture on the following page shows four pictures that depict the light position on the gun. One works well, the others not so much. I strongly recommend sticking to a six o'clock position if at all possible.

Figure 29 Light mounted on the left side of the rifle will illuminate and wash back into the operator's eyes when working the edge of a wall to the right.

Figure 28 Light mounted on the right side of the rifle will illuminate and wash back into the operator's eyes when working the edge of a wall to the left.

Figure 30 Light mounted at the 12 O'clock position will illuminate the smoke from the muzzle and make it very difficult to see the red dot.

Figure 14 Light mounted at the 6 O'clock position with the pressure activation switch on top of the handguard. This is the superior position to mount a light on a rifle if possible.

Light Use With a Rifle

If you have done your job of setting up the rifle properly and have a light mounted (at 6 o'clock) with an activation switch, using the light is easy and nothing really changes from your normal shooting positions. When I train with my rifle, I al-

ways utilize the same front hand position with my thumb riding the light switch even if I do not need the light. Consistency is the key here and I want to ensure I am practicing with a technique that will be consistent no matter what situation I

Figure 31 Notice the thumb on top of the light activation switch, where it stays consistently no matter what light condition I am training in.

am in.

Using your light should be simple, simply mount the rifle and squeeze the pressure activation switch and illuminate and shoot. Keep the light on after you are done shooting to ensure you have light to identify the actions of the threat.

Alternate Lighting Solutions

While you should always have a light mounted to your rifle, in some cases you may not...or it might stop working. What then? You need to have a solution for the rare cases your weapon mounted light is unusable. There are two primary techniques you can utilize in this case. The key in this situation is to practice with these techniques, and as always, if you do not have a handheld light on your person, you're in trouble! See the picture below for non-weapon mounted rifle lighting solutions.

Figure 32 Two options for a light solution if you DO NOT have a weapon mounted light on your rifle. Try them both and pick the best for you.

Low Light Rifle Closing Thoughts

The rifle is the ultimate defensive tool *if* you train with it. It seems that in the last few years with AR style rifle sales up simply because of fear, that there are a huge number of people that own one that have never taken the time to properly set up their rifle, let alone train with it. And using it in a low light situation is a completely different animal that daytime use. I am amazed at the number of students I have in classes with rifle light set ups that will likely be less than effective for their intended use, but have not taken the time to actually *shoot* their rifle at night.

The point? Make sure you are not assuming you will be able to simply grab your rifle and prevail with it is foolish at best. If you plan on using yours as a defensive tool, specifically a low light defensive tool, then you need to hit the range and shoot with it in the exact conditions that you expect to use it. Your eyes will be opened, and I would predict you will come to some of the same conclusions I have in terms of light and light switch mounting positions.

CHAPTER 10

Conclusion: Action Steps

While I hope you have learned from the chapters in this book, I wanted to end with a short discussion on *action*. The problem today is not the lack of information; it is the lack of *action on information*. I find myself watching television or following social media channels that report on the attack of the day, whether it be terrorism, crime related, or a crazy lunatic. The key is that each individual, each of you reading this must make a decision. That decision is

1. That you wish to defend yourself and others, and

2. That you will take action and prepare yourself to do so.

Without those two steps, nothing else matters. I have now authored four primary books on developing shooting skills, one of which was oriented toward the competition shooter. In a world where there are around 30,000 members of the practical shooting organizations and several million concealed carry permit holders you would expect me to sell many more of my defensive handgun training books than the competition book, wouldn't you? The truth is that the competition book (Your Competition Handgun Training Program) has and probably always will outsell the defensive books.

Why? I am not certain, but believe it is because the competition book fullfills material sought out by those with a passion for their hobby. Defensive training however seems to take a back seat in most peoples lives to their hobby (golf, nascar, fishing, who knows?).

Simply because you are reading this book, I know you are different. But that doesn't mean you are not human, as am I. So I write this end chapter with some actionable steps to follow, that if you do, you will be infinitely better at fighting in the low light environment than you were before. Here you go:

1. Reduce your low light exposure. This might include setting up motion-activated lights in your home and yard. Stick to well lit paths and parking lots.
2. Develop your fundamental handgun skills first, and carry a gun. If you are not spending at least two sessions a month practicing the basic skills I referenced via Tom Givens data, then you are probably short changing yourself to start working low light skills. Remember, prioritize, then execute.
3. Select the proper gear, and spend money on the best you can buy. I like the following:
    a. Streamlight TLR2HL for a full or midsized firearm with a weapon mounted light (make sure you get the contoured pressure activation switch).
    b. Streamlight Protac 1L or Klarus XTC1 for handheld lights.
    c. Streamlight Protac Rail Mount 1 for rifle weapon mounted lights. I am also very intrigued by the Crimson Trace LINQ system (a wireless rifle mounted light) but have NOT tested it yet.
    d. The Streamlight TLR-6 or the Streamlight Laserguard Pro (a light laser combination) for smaller, carry guns.
4. Start your low light training by getting practicing your light and tactical techniques in your own home with a training gun (red plastic gun or S.I.R.T pistol) and no live firearms. You will learn more from this type of practice than almost anything else. Step up your game by adding a live human you have to find and react to.
5. Add skills like defending your head and striking to your skillset. Practice striking with your light on a heavy bag or similar, and buy a set of cheap boxing gloves and have a friend throw a few punches at you so you can practice caging and defending your head.
6. Hit the range at least once a month with your all of your low light gear. Practice with weapon mounted lights and handheld lights and work the live fire drills in this book. Add more drills as you grow comfortable. Bring your rifle with light if you have one.
    a. Note: If you can not find a suitable live fire range, utilize the dry fire drills provided.

7. Take a low light class or visit www.americanwarriorsociety.com or Vimeo (search low light) for videos on the material covered in this book if you are a visual learner.

There you have it! A simple checklist to get yourself moving toward a higher level of skill. Remember, the first step is making the decision to act, and once you have done that, the rest will fall into place! And remember –

The Fight's Coming – Are you Ready?

Mike Seeklander

ABOUT THE AUTHOR

Currently Mike Seeklander is owner of Shooting-Performance LLC (www.shooting-performance.com), a full service training company and the American Warrior Society, the most comprehensive source of self-defense information on the internet (www.americanwarriorsociety.com). Mike is also the co-host of The Best Defense, the Outdoor Channels leading self-defense and firearm instruction show.

From 1995-98, I was employed by the Knox County (TN) Sheriff's Department's Corrections division and was a member of its highly trained Special Operations Response Team. From 1998-2001, I worked as a police officer for the Knoxville (TN) Police Department where I was assigned as a patrol officer and also as an investigator for the Organized Crime section, investigating narcotics and vice-related crimes at the local, state and federal levels.

After that, as an employee of the federal government, Mike served as the Branch Chief and Lead Instructor for the Firearms division with the Federal Air Marshal Service as well as a Senior Instructor at the Federal Law Enforcement Training Center (F.L.E.T.C.), the premier federal training facility in the U.S. Mike has extensive formal training and experience in all phases of military and law enforcement training and is a highly sought after defensive and competitive trainer.

Following his federal career, Mike was Chief Operating Officer, Director of Training, and a Senior Instructor at the U.S. Shooting Academy in Tulsa, OK.

He was directly responsible for the development of more than fifty firearm-training programs.

Currently a nationally ranked competitor on the practical handgun competition circuit, Seeklander has authored/produced instructional books, DVD's and has developed hundreds of lesson plans specifically related to both basic and advanced firearms training.

Mike is the recipient of numerous awards and honors in the law enforcement community, and as a semi-professional shooter. Mike is the 2013 and 2014 I.D.P.A. B.U.G. (Back up Gun) national champion, winner of the 2011 Steel Challenge World Speed Shooting Championships (production division title), and numerous state and area championships. The United States Practical Shooting Association currently ranks Mike as a Grandmaster. Having competed in the shooting sports nationally, Mike adds to this experience with more than 20 years of experience in various martial arts holding multiple ranks including a Black Belt in Okinawan Freestyle Karate.

Mike is a combat veteran of Desert Shield and Desert Storm, with five years of active duty and four years of reserve duty in the U.S. Marine Corps, as an intelligence specialist and primary marksmanship instructor, and combat engineer. Prior to receiving my honorable discharge in 2000, he was attached to a Federal multi-agency task force investigating large-scale international drug trafficking in Los Angeles, CA.

Made in the USA
Columbia, SC
11 February 2019